NAVY SEALS

by Kristin Marciniak

Content Consultant
James C. Bradford
Professor of History
Texas A&M University

CORE
LIBRARY

Published by ABDO Publishing Company, PO Box 398166, Minneapolis, MN 55439. Copyright © 2013 by Abdo Consulting Group, Inc. International copyrights reserved in all countries. No part of this book may be reproduced in any form without written permission from the publisher. The Core Library™ is a trademark and logo of ABDO Publishing Company.

Printed in the United States of America,
North Mankato, Minnesota
112012
012013

♻ THIS BOOK CONTAINS AT LEAST 10% RECYCLED MATERIALS.

Editor: Lauren Coss
Series Designer: Becky Daum

Cataloging-in-Publication Data
Marciniak, Kristin.
 Navy SEALS / Kristin Marciniak.
   p. cm. -- (Great warriors)
Includes bibliographical references and index.
ISBN 978-1-61783-725-8
1. United States. Navy. SEALS--Juvenile literature. 2. United States. Navy-
-Commando troops--Juvenile literature. 3. Special operations (Military
science)--Juvenile literature. 1. Title.
359.9/84--dc22
                                                    2012946370

Photo Credits: Schalk van Zuydam/AP Images, cover, 1; George R. Kusner/U.S. Navy/Getty Images, 4; AP Images, 7, 14, 17, 18, 20; CIA/AP Images, 8; The White House, Pete Souza/AP Images, 10; PO1 Michelle Turner/US Navy, 12; US Navy/AP Images, 23, 25; Milton R. Savage/US Navy/Time Life Pictures/Getty Images, 27; Stocktrek Images/Thinkstock, 28, 34, 45; MC2 Kyle D. Gahlau/US Navy, 30; JOCS Lee Coleman/US Navy, 37; SGT Derek Kuhn/US Army, 38; U.S. Navy, Lance H. Mayhew Jr./AP Images, 40

CONTENTS

CHAPTER ONE

TARGET: BIN LADEN

It was May 1, 2011. Two Black Hawk helicopters sped quietly through the dark skies of Afghanistan. Inside, an elite team of warriors prepared for its next strike. The team's destination was Abbottabad, Pakistan.

This was no ordinary military team. These men were US Navy SEALs. They were some of the toughest troops in the world. And this was no ordinary mission.

US Navy SEALs take on some of the toughest and most dangerous missions in the world.

The SEALs' mission was to capture or kill a man named Osama bin Laden. He was the leader of a terrorist group that had attacked the United States on September 11, 2001. The SEALs' target was a compound in an Abbottabad neighborhood. They thought that bin Laden was hiding there.

Four Chinook helicopters followed the two Black Hawks. The Chinooks carried 25 more SEALs. If the first team had problems escaping, this backup team would help.

The first Black Hawk was supposed to hover

September 11 Attacks

A terrorist group attacked the United States on September 11, 2001. Members of the group hijacked airplanes. Then the group crashed the planes into the World Trade Center in New York City and the Pentagon in Washington DC. A fourth hijacked plane crashed in a field in Pennsylvania. This plane never reached the hijackers' intended destination. A group called al-Qaeda claimed responsibility for the attacks. Osama bin Laden was the group's leader.

US forces hunted Osama bin Laden for nearly ten years after the 2001 terrorist attacks on the United States.

over the compound. Then the SEALs would slide down a rope. The pilot tried hovering. But he lost control of the helicopter. It hit a wall and crashed to the ground. The SEALs hit the ground running. The mission was not supposed to go this way.

The second Black Hawk pilot saw the first Black Hawk crash. He landed his helicopter in a grassy field

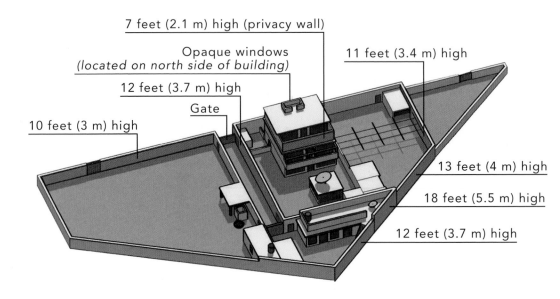

7 feet (2.1 m) high (privacy wall)

Opaque windows
(located on north side of building)

11 feet (3.4 m) high

12 feet (3.7 m) high

Gate

10 feet (3 m) high

13 feet (4 m) high

18 feet (5.5 m) high

12 feet (3.7 m) high

The Abbottabad Compound

This diagram shows the layout of the compound where bin Laden was hiding. After reading about the compound, what did you imagine it looked like? How has that idea changed? How does seeing the compound help you better understand the SEALs' attack on it?

across the street. The SEALs from the second Black Hawk hurried to join their teammates.

The SEALs ran through thick mud toward the house. They used explosives to blast through the gates. They cleared the first floor of the three-story house. They used more explosives to get through the gates to the second floor. No one was there. They went up to the third floor.

At the top of the stairs, the lead SEAL spotted a man peeking out from behind a bedroom door. The man was tall and thin. He had a long beard. The SEAL recognized the man through his night-vision goggles. It was Osama bin Laden.

There are different accounts of what happened when the SEALs spotted bin Laden. According to one account, the SEALs rushed into the bedroom. Two of bin Laden's wives stood in front of him. A SEAL grabbed the two women. He wrapped his arms around them to make sure they were not wearing any explosives.

Bin Laden was now in full view. A SEAL shot bin Laden in the head and the chest before he could reach for a weapon.

Night-Vision Goggles

The Black Hawk pilots didn't turn on the headlights as they were flying into the compound. It was important that no one saw the Black Hawks. Instead, the pilots and the SEALs wore night-vision goggles so they could safely navigate their way to the target. Night-vision goggles help SEALs see in the dark.

President Barack Obama edits his speech before making a televised statement announcing bin Laden's death.

Nine years, seven months, and twenty days after the attacks on the United States, bin Laden was dead. The US Navy SEALs had been on the ground for only 40 minutes.

On May 1, 2011, President Barack Obama gave a speech announcing that US Navy SEALs had killed Osama bin Laden:

> Today, at my direction, the United States launched a targeted operation against that compound in Abbottabad, Pakistan. A small team of Americans carried out the operation with extraordinary courage and capability. No Americans were harmed. They took care to avoid civilian casualties. After a firefight, they killed Osama bin Laden and took custody of his body. . . .
>
> The death of bin Laden marks the most significant achievement to date in our nation's effort to defeat al Qaeda. . . . Yet his death does not mark the end of our effort. . . . We must—and we will—remain vigilant at home and abroad.

Source: *The White House.* The White House Blog, May 2, 2011. Web. Accessed August 7, 2012.

Consider Your Audience

Read Obama's speech closely. How could you adapt the speech for a different audience, such as your parents or younger friends? Write a blog post conveying this same information for the new audience. What is the best way to get your point across to this audience?

CHAPTER TWO

WAGING WAR FROM THE WATER

US Navy SEALs are a part of the Naval Special Warfare Command. This is a branch of the US Navy. The SEALs got their name because of the places they work: Sea, Air, and Land. Today there are 2,400 active-duty SEALs. They are deployed to 30 countries around the world.

The SEALs weren't always a part of the US Navy. In fact, the SEALs as we know them today

Navy SEALs have been a part of every major US conflict in the past 50 years.

Amphibious warfare involves launching attacks on land from ships at sea.

were not created until the early 1960s. But there has always been a need for military forces that are skilled in amphibious attacks. These forces were able to land and operate successfully in both land and water missions. Those teams' experiences led to the creation of the US Navy SEALs.

World War II

The US Navy and Marine Corps developed amphibious landing techniques in the 1930s. These skills included finding beaches that were good for landing and looking for enemy forces. These techniques also covered getting rid of any mines or dangerous obstacles and guiding small boats safely to shore.

Dangerous Mines

Enemy mines made troop landings difficult. These mines were usually large poles rooted in the sand and pointed out to sea. The top of the pole looked like a mushroom. The mine exploded if the pole was hit. The mines prevented ships from getting close to the beach. They also made it hard for armored vehicles, such as tanks, to land.

These amphibious tactics were helpful when the United States entered World War II (1939–1945) in 1941. The battles against the Japanese in the Pacific Ocean took place entirely on islands. US enemies, known as the Axis powers, controlled Western Europe. The first American troops to invade the

D-Day

The largest amphibious assault in history took place on June 6, 1944, known as D-Day. This was the day US forces and their allies invaded the beaches of Normandy, France. Members of the US Navy had been preparing for this invasion for weeks. The beaches of Normandy already looked like a war zone before any soldiers landed. Amphibious forces figured out how to get past deadly mines. They made sure the water along the beaches was deep enough for landing. They also tested sand samples. They needed to make sure the beaches could support the tanks and other heavy vehicles coming to shore. Thanks to the hard work of the navy's amphibious forces, D-Day was a success for the United States and its allies.

continent had to land from ships at sea.

The navy's job was to transport and protect the troops arriving by sea. Landing a ship on a beach was very dangerous. An enemy could spot a huge ship from miles away. Mines and other dangerous structures prevented ships from getting close. It was safer to keep the ships away from the shore and move troops to shore in small boats.

Those early landings were often costly. Many men were killed. Lots of

US troops arrive by sea on the beaches off the coast of France on D-Day, June 6, 1944.

supplies were lost. Navy officials realized amphibious landings required special training. A new military force was needed.

Special Teams

The Scouts and Raiders were the first in a line of teams that led to the Navy SEALs. The Scouts and Raiders were created in 1942. Their mission was reconnaissance, or gathering information. They searched beaches and shorelines before an invasion.

An Underwater Demolition Team uses explosives to clear the coastline of a Pacific island before a 1944 beach landing.

They were looking for good places to land. Then they set up signaling locations. This way they could guide the landing boats safely to shore. The Scouts and Raiders worked at night so the enemy would not see them.

Another unit, called the Navy Combat Demolition Unit (NCDU), was created in June 1943. These men were in charge of clearing the beaches of mines and other obstacles before the troops arrived.

The navy also had to deal with dangers under the water. The Underwater Demolition Teams (UDTs) were created in November 1943. UDTs made sure underwater mines or dangerous coral reefs would not harm arriving troops.

NCDUs and UDTs played an important role in winning World War II. More than 3,500 NCDUs and UDTs had seen combat by the time Japan surrendered on September 2, 1945. These teams were valuable members of the US military. But something still seemed to be missing.

EXPLORE ONLINE

The Web site below has even more information about the amphibious teams of World War II. As you know, every source is different. Reread Chapter Two of this book. What are the similarities between Chapter Two and the information you found on the Web site? Are there any differences? How do the two sources present information differently?

Naval Special Warfare Command
www.public.navy.mil/nsw/pages/History.aspx

CHAPTER THREE

NAVY SEALS IN VIETNAM AND BEYOND

The early 1960s were an important time for the navy's amphibious troops. The United States entered the Vietnam War (1954–1975) in 1961. North Vietnam was trying to take over South Vietnam. The North Vietnamese were using guerrilla warfare. This type of warfare involves unexpected attacks by an unofficial military group. The United States supported South Vietnam in the conflict.

Navy SEALs played an important role in the US military's involvement in the Vietnam War.

An Unusual War

The fighting in Vietnam was not a style of fighting the US Army was used to. Combat took place in jungles instead of on traditional battlefields. US forces often couldn't see the enemy they were fighting. President John F. Kennedy wanted to create a special unit that would be specially trained to fight this type of war. It would be broken up into smaller units. These small units could move easily over the rough landscape. The UDTs already knew how to work in small units. They became the foundation for the US Navy SEALs.

The UDTs were already working along the coast of Vietnam. They looked for underwater obstacles and kept track of the tides. They were not trained in guerrilla warfare.

President John. F. Kennedy wanted the navy to create a special new unit. This new unit would use unconventional warfare tactics. Military officials agreed. The US Navy SEALs were born.

SEALs in Vietnam

The military created US Navy SEAL Teams 1 and 2 in January 1962. The first units went to Vietnam in 1963. Their mission was to respond to guerrilla warfare.

US Navy SEALs worked in the jungles and along the coasts and rivers of Vietnam.

They would conduct secret operations in ocean or river environments.

At first the SEALs were not allowed to go on operations into North Vietnam. Instead, they taught South Vietnamese soldiers how to fight in and along the water. SEALs also spent time helping US troops get used to living and fighting in the jungle.

SEALs were used more and more for combat as the war went on. They fought against North Vietnamese soldiers and their South Vietnamese allies, who were known as the Vietcong. The SEALs raided enemy camps. They cut off Vietcong communications and destroyed their weapons. They also closed down the routes used to transport supplies to the Vietcong.

The SEALs also worked to free South Vietnamese prisoners of war. They rescued pilots whose planes had been shot down in the jungle. These were dangerous

Bravery in Action

Navy SEAL Lieutenant Joseph Robert "Bob" Kerrey was part of SEAL Team 1 stationed in Vietnam. On March 14, 1969, Kerrey was leading his squad against the Vietcong when a grenade exploded at his feet. He was badly hurt. He eventually lost his leg due to injuries from the explosion. But he still led his men to safety. On May 14, 1970, Kerrey became the first US Navy SEAL to earn the Medal of Honor. The Medal of Honor is the highest award a US military member can earn. It honors bravery against an enemy force.

Members of SEAL Team 1 travel down a river in Vietnam.

missions. The SEALs had gone through special training back home, but they had never fought in a jungle before. They had to develop new tactics and techniques. They were always learning on the job.

At one point, more than 200 SEALs were deployed to Vietnam. Several hundred more SEALs were training at home. But the US Navy left the war in 1973. After that, there wasn't a need for so many

SEALs to be on active duty. Some retired. Others moved to different areas of the navy.

Some SEALs stayed active during this time. In the 1980s, the SEALs' goals were expanded. They helped other parts of the navy by gathering information. They performed sneak attacks on ships in harbors. But SEALs would be involved in a war again soon.

Back in Action

In 1990 Iraq invaded its neighboring country Kuwait. The invasion triggered the Persian Gulf War (1990–1991). The United States and its allies got involved in the conflict. US Navy SEALs set up a military base in the region. As the war went on, the SEALs found themselves doing many of the tasks they had done in earlier wars. They rescued pilots whose planes had crashed. They destroyed enemy mines. SEALs studied the coastline to prepare for invasions. They also helped train the Kuwaiti navy to fight against Iraqi forces.

SEAL Team 8 trains for a mission in the Persian Gulf War.

SEALs Today

After the 2001 attacks on the United States, the US Navy SEALs became fully committed to fighting terrorist groups around the world. They use raids to steal their enemies' weapons. They also attack enemy property. They help free hostages.

Just as in the early days of the Scouts and Raiders, today's SEALs also do a lot of reconnaissance. They gather information about the enemy. They learn

Today's US Navy SEALs travel all over the world. One of their main missions is to fight back against terrorist groups.

where the enemy is hiding and what it is planning to do next. They study shore and water conditions before beach landings. They find out as much information as they can before a mission begins.

Since the Vietnam War, US Navy SEALs have rescued hostages and protected government officials. SEALs are deployed to approximately 30 countries around the world. A team is always nearby if a conflict arises. A team of SEALs can be put into action faster than any other US military organization. But not just anybody can be a US Navy SEAL.

FURTHER EVIDENCE

There was quite a bit of information about US Navy SEALs in Chapter Three. But if you could pick out the main point of the chapter, what would it be? What evidence was given to support that point? Visit the Web site below to learn more about the SEALs' attitude and way of life. Choose a quote from the Web site that relates to Chapter Three. Does this quote support the author's main point? Or does it make a new point? Write a few sentences explaining how the quote you found relates to Chapter Three.

Ethos

www.sealswcc.com/navy-seals-ethos.aspx

CHAPTER FOUR

A SEAL'S LIFE

Navy SEALs are not your average soldiers. They spend hours each day doing physical training. They have excellent teamwork skills and strong self-esteem. Becoming a SEAL is not easy. Many men try to complete the training. But only one out of every four trainees becomes a US Navy SEAL.

Navy SEALs are incredible athletes who undergo an extremely tough training program.

Becoming a SEAL

Not everyone can qualify to become a SEAL. Training is open only to men enlisted in the US Navy who are younger than 29 years old. Training to become a US Navy SEAL begins at the Naval Special Warfare Preparatory School in Great Lakes, Illinois. The two-month-long program helps prepare people who might become US Navy SEALs. Potential SEALs practice running, swimming, and other exercises. Trainees must pass a physical screening test at the end of the course. They will not be able to continue with SEAL training if they don't pass. They will be given other jobs in the navy instead.

Trainees who pass the physical screening test move to the Naval Special Warfare Center in Coronado, California. Then it's time for Basic Underwater Demolition/SEALs training (BUD/S). BUD/S is very tough. Fifty percent of trainees drop out before the six-month class is over.

	US Navy SEAL	Special Warfare Combatant-craft Crewmen	Explosive Ordnance Disposal	Diver	Aviation Rescue Swimmer
Mission	Engage in unconventional warfare on sea, air, and land.	Operate small craft used in special operations missions, especially Navy SEAL missions.	Destroy or disarm explosive weapons.	Perform underwater salvage, repair, maintenance, and rescues.	Perform search and rescue missions in all environments
Swim 500 yards (400 m) (in minutes)	12:30	13:00	14:00	14:00	12:00
Rest: 10 Minutes					
Push-ups (in 2 minutes)	42	42	42	42	42
Rest: 2 Minutes					
Sit-ups (in 2 minutes)	50	50	50	50	50
Rest: 2 Minutes					
Pull-ups (in 2 minutes)	6	6	6	6	4
Rest: 10 Minutes					
Run 1.5 Miles (2.4 km) (in minutes)	11:00	12:30	12:45	12:45	12:00

SEAL Physical Screening Test Requirements

This chart shows the minimum scores needed to pass the navy physical screening test. Only men who far exceed these scores will be accepted into the SEAL training program. How do the scores to become a SEAL compare with the scores for other positions in the navy? How might these scores relate to each position's mission? How does the information in the chart help you understand the information in this chapter? How does the information in this chapter help you understand the chart?

Navy SEALs train to battle the surf in small rubber boats.

BUD/S has four parts: Basic Orientation, First Phase, Second Phase, and Third Phase. Basic Orientation is three weeks long. It prepares potential SEALs for the physical training in First Phase. It also helps the men become familiar with the obstacle course and the small rubber boats they use.

First Phase

First Phase is seven weeks long. It focuses on teamwork, swimming and water skills, and physical training. Trainees have to be in good shape at the beginning of this phase. SEAL trainees swim two miles (3.2 km) in the ocean, run four miles (6.4 km) on the beach, and complete an obstacle course. As First Phase continues, the daily activity becomes longer and longer. Trainees must do the run, swim, and obstacle course in even less time.

Second Phase

Second Phase is seven weeks long. During this phase, trainees learn the underwater skills SEALs need to know. The men will be able to stay underwater for a full minute by the end of Second Phase. They even practice staying underwater with their hands and feet tied together.

The trainees practice diving in a 50-foot (15.2 m) diving tower filled with 110,000 gallons (416,000 L) of water. The bottom of the tank has a submarine lockout chamber. The men learn how to enter and exit a submarine while it is underwater.

Hell Week

The fourth week of First Phase is the hardest week of all. This part of the training is known as Hell Week. The goal of Hell Week is to push every trainee further than he thinks he can go. For five and a half days, the men run, swim, row, and trudge through the mud. The men average only about an hour of sleep each night. They usually sleep in the sand, mud, or water. They are not allowed to stop for sickness or injuries. These conditions may seem unfair or even dangerous. But they are necessary. Life as a US Navy SEAL is not easy. The men need to be prepared for what lies ahead.

Third Phase and SQT

Third Phase is the final phase of BUD/S training. This is when SEAL trainees learn how to work with explosives and use weapons. They study reconnaissance, navigation, small-unit tactics, and patrolling techniques.

Men who finish the seven-week Third Phase are not US Navy SEALs quite yet. They still need to complete SEAL Qualification Training,

For most Navy SEALs, First Phase's Hell Week is the most difficult part of their training.

or SQT. In SQT trainees learn more about weapons, navigation, and small-unit tactics. They also receive cold-weather training and learn medical skills. They even learn how to parachute out of an airplane.

The men must complete one final training before graduating from SQT. They must pass Survival, Evasion, Resistance, and Escape (SERE) training. SERE makes sure the trainees know what to do if an enemy captures them. The trainees are dropped off in the desert. They first need to survive without any food or water. Then their instructors capture them.

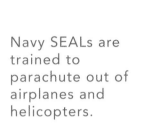

Navy SEALs are trained to parachute out of airplanes and helicopters.

The instructors pretend to be the enemy. The men must not give up any information when they are captured. The SEAL trainees need to prove they can live up to the US military's Code of Conduct.

Candidates who complete SQT are now officially US Navy SEALs. These new SEALs are assigned to one of nine SEAL teams. Then they begin preparing for their first deployment.

Brotherhood of SEALs

Navy SEAL training centers on teamwork and trust. This focus builds a strong bond between men in the same platoon or team. The team is everything to the SEALs. A US Navy SEAL never leaves a teammate behind, even if he is injured or has died.

Every team member is assigned a specific duty. It is important for the SEALs to stick to those roles. Everyone has a job to do to keep the team safe. If a SEAL is killed or wounded, somebody has done something wrong.

There is no other combat unit quite like the US Navy SEALs. They are strong, smart, and brave men. SEALs risk their lives

Platoons

Today's SEALs are divided into nine teams. Each SEAL team has six platoons. Each platoon usually has two officers, one chief, and thirteen enlisted men. Two platoons from each team are deployed at a time. Platoons are deployed to different places around the world. They are stationed on ships, submarines, aircraft carriers, and military bases overseas. Deployments are usually six to eight months long.

One of the US Navy SEALs' most important principles is to never leave a man behind.

for the United States every day. Sixty years after their creation, the US Navy SEALs continue to work hard. They are making the United States and the world a safer place.

Bob Schoultz is a retired US Navy SEAL and Naval Special Warfare officer. He wrote the following passage as part of an essay for *Ethos*, the US Navy SEALs' magazine.

> *Resilience, like many things, is both simple and complex. In essence, it seems to come down to an ability to cope and respond well to adversity and stress. The opposite of resilience might be fragile, rigid or delicate. . . . The most resilient warriors have confronted physical fear and risk of failure by training under varied and challenging conditions. The most resilient managers have sought and confronted new administrative challenges in unfamiliar settings. The most resilient families are willing to try new approaches or call on professional counseling when communications break down and relationships are in jeopardy. All of these involve bending to new challenges, and confronting and working through discomfort and even fear.*

> *Source: Bob Schoultz. "Resilience." Ethos July/August 2011: 28. PDF. Accessed September 20, 2012.*

Changing Minds

This passage discusses resilience. Take a position on resilience and its importance for US Navy SEAL teams. Then imagine that your best friend has the opposite opinion. Write a short essay trying to change your friend's mind. Make sure you explain your opinion and your reasons for it.

IMPORTANT DATES AND BATTLES

1941

The United States enters World War II.

1942

The US military creates the Scout and Raiders.

1943

The navy creates the Navy Combat Demolition Unit (NCDU) in June.

1962

The military creates US SEAL Teams 1 and 2 in January.

1963

The first SEALs are deployed to Vietnam to help fight in the Vietnam War.

1973

The US Navy leaves Vietnam, taking the SEALs with them.

1943

The navy creates the first Underwater Demolition Team (UDT) in November.

1944

On June 6, US forces and their allies invade the beaches of Normandy, France. The invasion becomes known as D-Day.

1961

President John F. Kennedy calls for an increase in unconventional warfare units, triggering the development of the US Navy SEALs program.

1990

Iraqi forces invade Kuwait. SEALs set up a military base in the region.

2001

A terrorist group led by Osama bin Laden attacks the United States on September 11.

2011

On May 1, US Navy SEALs kill Osama bin Laden in Abbottabad, Pakistan.

Why Do I Care?

A US Navy SEAL's life can be pretty tough and exciting. Your life might be similar to a SEAL's in ways you might not have thought of. Have you ever worked hard for a sport or activity? Have you ever been a part of a team and had to put the team's goals before your own? Write down two or three ways US Navy SEALs connect to your life.

Dig Deeper

What questions do you still have about US Navy SEALs? Do you want to learn more about their training? Or their missions? Write down one or two questions that can guide you in doing research. With an adult's help, find a few reliable new sources about US Navy SEALs that can help answer your questions. Write a few sentences about how you did your research and what you learned from it.

Surprise Me

Learning about US Navy SEALs can be interesting and surprising. Think about what you learned from this book. Can you name the two or three facts in this book that you found most surprising? Write a short paragraph about each. Describe what you found surprising and why.

Take a Stand

Take a position on the use of SEALs in combat. Then write a short essay explaining your opinion. Make sure you give reasons for your opinion. Give some evidence to support those reasons.

GLOSSARY

amphibious
designed for operation on or from both water and land

combat
armed fighting

compound
a cluster of homes, often owned by members of the same family

deployed
ready for use in action

elite
the best of a group

guerrilla warfare
unexpected attacks by an unofficial military group

navigate
direct or manage a ship, aircraft, guided missile, group, or individual on its course

obstacle
something that stands in the way of progress

raid
a sudden attack on the enemy

reconnaissance
the act of searching for information about the enemy

tactics
plans

unconventional
not bound by traditional rules or restrictions

LEARN MORE

Books

Hamilton, John. *Navy SEALs*. Edina, MN: ABDO, 2012.

Kennedy, Robert C. *Life with the Navy SEALs*. New York: Children's Press, 2000.

Lusted, Marcia Amidon. *The Capture and Killing of Osama bin Laden*. Edina, MN: ABDO, 2011.

Web Links

To learn more about US Navy SEALs, visit ABDO Publishing Company online at **www.abdopublishing.com.** Web sites about SEALs are featured on our Book Links page. These links are routinely monitored and updated to provide the most current information available.

Visit **www.mycorelibrary.com** for free additional tools for teachers and students.

INDEX

ABOUT THE AUTHOR

Kristin Marciniak grew up in Bettendorf, Iowa. She graduated from the University of Missouri–Columbia with a bachelor's degree in journalism. Today, she lives in Kansas City, Missouri, with her husband, her son, and a very friendly golden retriever. She likes to read, write, knit, and sew.